EYE TO EYE

Peter Fallon

EYE TO EYE

for Sarah and Peter and, when the time comes, Fiachra and Clíodhna —

Peter
Loughcrew '92

Gallery Books

Eye to Eye
is first published
simultaneously in paperback
and in a clothbound edition
on 30 October 1992.

The Gallery Press
Loughcrew
Oldcastle
County Meath
Ireland

*All rights reserved. For permission
to reprint or broadcast these poems,
write to The Gallery Press.*

© Peter Fallon 1992

ISBN 1 85235 100 4 (*paperback*)
    1 85235 101 2 (*clothbound*)

The Gallery Press receives financial assistance from An Chomhairle
Ealaíon / The Arts Council, Ireland.

Contents

A Woman of the Fields *page* 11
Annaghmakerrig: The Avenue 12
The Woman of the House 14
Eye to Eye 16
Windfalls 19
Gravities: West 20
The A.G.M. 21
The State of the Nation 22
Possessed 24
Holidays 29
A Handful of Air 30
One Day 32
The Wife 33
Omega House 34
Seven Letters Beginning With . . . 36
Fast 43
The River 44
Big 46
Winds and Weathers 48
Grace 50
A Way of the World 52
The World of Women 53
A Part of Ourselves 54

Acknowledgements 62

*in memory of John Fallon
born 7 December
died 8 December 1990*

A Woman of the Fields

She stands in the middle of a field
and says she'll stand there
for years.

— But come the summer
and the mower's path?
She'll be grass.

— Come Autumn
and the chainsaw's teeth?
She'll be wood.

— And Winter?
She'll be fodder, fruit of fields.
Spring she'll grow again.

She'll grow again I know.
An other woman
shades my meadow

and I mind this:
a blade of her hair in a book
and her big kiss.

Annaghmakerrig: The Avenue

He's been at it
all week —
scything the grass by the avenue.
We greet each other when we pass,
but he doesn't speak.

Maybe I say 'Grand day'
or 'Mighty weather' as I go by,
but he keeps looking away.
There's a nod or a wink.
We've never exactly seen eye to eye.

I work by a long bay window
and he's there, a human pendulum,
a metronome, at it all day.
I wake to the sound of his effortless
swing and swish. I hear his hum

when I dander down in the afternoon
to the water's
edge where a woman shared her story
of how black the dark can be,
the force of depression before her daughter's

birth; and coming back,
my grim reaper —
as I walk weighed with privilege
and buoyant with the ceremony
of her gift — my tight keeper

of his own counsel, is waiting.
Waiting. Was he one of the twin brothers
who served time in Portlaoise
for the murder of a Protestant
or one of the others

from the next townland
where — I'm told —
a Catholic never slept a night,
all of them training on a FÁS scheme
to put to right the old

demesne? Forget, forgive,
turn the other cheek . . . .
He is gradually cutting his way
uphill towards the house. Morning,
noon or night he doesn't speak.

No, not a word. But he smiles.

The Woman of the House

It's not that I minded at first.
God knows the warm word
was welcome.
Such thoughts — and me my age.
Soft talk and silly sayings slurred

into rough touch.
He'd push and forage
and him back from the town
and not within an ass's roar of himself.
Was this his notion of a marriage?

Was this why I stayed home?
As long as I draw breath
I'll ask myself
is this the cross I earned?
Sometimes I'd wish I was for death.

And none to tell a thing
except himself, my own brother.
We'd been so close
we'd eaten off one plate.
It got so bad the other

night I had to go out
to the shed.
Again. Then the world was draughts
and shadows, a bar of light
beneath the kitchen door, an unsaid

worry. I waited there
an age until his ravings ended.
Then he began to snore
and I stole home to say my prayers.
The peace of sleep ascended.

Eye to Eye

Grain on the roadside,
small change of a fortune;

his geese are gone from goslings.

> ∾

He has pitched his fill.
He is leaning against the tailboard
of a low trailer:

'The man who couldn't save hay
the year
needs help with more than the baler.'

> ∾

He worked with
and not against the weather.
A happy man.
Trade is good and the grass
is gone. The last time we were together

at a harvest dance,
his silhouette in
a lather of sweat
marvelled at the size of the crowd.
You'd need a haircut to get in.

The full of the hall and more
in the yard. When he'd shaken
and held my partner's hand
he turned to enquire,
'Is this the wife, or grass you've taken?'

◈

You never paid me for mowing
the barley
that time you were wanting to reap.

Would you call that mowing?
It was barely topped. I'd to cut it
again to count the sheep.

◈

He stares at it, eye to eye,
the storm;
the man who cuts winter wood's
twice warm.

◈

I'll bale for you surely
if you're sure,
but is the bottoms wet?
It's not so bad — nothing a wipe
of that wind won't cure.

Would I want to wear boots,
boots or waders? Ah quit.
It's hardly a graveyard.
If you venture there
you'll get out of it.

         ත ත

The whitethorn's as green
as the black —
he has broadcast seed
from an old sack-

apron and is taking
his ease.
Not in thunder or lightning,
he sees the bounty of God in a breeze.

Windfalls

He is foddering cattle at a gap,
the windiest part of the field.
They were giving out a gale last night,
strong westerlies and warnings.
'That's the wind that peeled

potatoes in New York!'
It skimmed the top of the Atlantic
and tipped it over Ireland.
The blue twine of a bale
is slicing perished fingers. Some antic

power flipped a roof into an outfield;
an undressed outhouse shivers by its edge.
The dervish dance of sleet and hail
has crusted backs of sheep,
cruel comfort by a whitethorn hedge.

Wild days and wicked weather
cut to the bone — not a lot to set store
by. They're troubled times.
'True. They're troubled times.
There's men dying now never died before.'

He has seen it all and lived to tell.
A cloudbreak lightens his eyes' frown.
'Don't fear or fret. They made the back
to bear the burden.' He'll saw and split
the windfalls when the wind dies down.

Gravities: West

She is stationed between
a briary
bush and a mountainy ash in the hedge
by the edge of bare grazing,
her eyes to high

heaven, her lamb
nibbling nothing, till they bend
in the breeze and she crops
from wild, western commonage
windfalls that depend

on whatever way that wind blows.

The A.G.M.

His suit doesn't fit,
his tie's too tight.
He knows the sun and the stars
shine in other places
but he doesn't feel right

at the Pedigree Sales,
the Charollais Association dinner,
or the Texel Society A.G.M.
He'd sooner be tangling over stock
where there's hardly a sinner

in shot of an ear or in sight,
or at the turn of a lane
for the setting of meadows. That field's
in great heart; they were always
kind acres — his undisturbed train

of thought. Remember the way he'd let on
to be buying a beast and then sell two?
As if home were a place
and not a time, in a car in the carpark
after the mart, he'd tell you

himself, That's better,
now I know where I am —
where his tongue belongs to the small talk,
the giving out, the praises, say,
of that Charley heifer or that Textile ram.

The State of the Nation

He was saying
they stick a tape across the eyes
before they pull the trigger.
So your man won't see?
No. So that when he dies

those eyes won't splash
out of his head
all over the place. They snapped off
fingers with bolt-cutters
and left a body dying or dead

in an open ditch.
Where? Somewhere
along the border. It doesn't matter
where exactly. At the end of the day
it's neither here nor there.

The eyes offended
and they plucked them out.
A hand offended . . . . They cut it
away. And the ring of truth
on the other hand. There's little doubt

they're not only up or over there.
There's men round here as bad
with their blather about Ireland.
Ireland. Poor and lovely
Ireland. They're mad

in the head, brave boys
in the dark, bright sparks
and the blind eye turned.
Draw them out; all they'll say
is, 'Pass no remarks'.

It'd make you spit blood.
If they so much
as shook your hand
you'd have to count your fingers,
limp men leaning on the crutch

of a crippled history.
And maybe they only drove a lorry
with nitrogen bags
on a dummy run to an arms dump
in a disused quarry

or gestured at a funeral
or touted *An Phoblacht*
in a decent pub.
If their day comes
the country's fucked.

Too much, too long,
their carry on as if it's playing
or play-acting. And you mean to say
no one knows who they are?
I mean to say no one's saying.

Possessed

They have made halves of themselves
to manage and have chosen a spot
without a thought
to dangle on the nub of one same branch
twines of bales by the knot

where they tend winter stock,
a cow that calved. They've dragged hay
and water down a right
of way. Cat's cradles wave in the wind.
They'll have made by March a May-

pole — if they live that long.

For weeks he has watched
the orange, blue and yellow
cords fly like ensigns at the border
of his grazing and as he has watched
he has felt a seed grow

in the mind. For every word
in his house was a nudge
of neighbours' trespass and transgression,
of wrongs done and disputes, and every look
was fuel on the fire of a grudge.

It wasn't off the ground he licked it.

No, that row started on the Ark. But was he
ever all right in the head? He was erratic,
but if you owed him money
he'd be right enough. He didn't know
the end of strength. Remember he'd be acrobatic

in a pub or public place — handstands,
cartwheels for a pound. A rush of blood
was little wonder
the way that he was pushed. And he began to plan
the end of them whose family name was mud

the morning something snapped.

For the broody mind must hatch.
And so he planted in a ditch
himself and all he needed — lock,
stock, and barrel, and a cartridge belt.
'I'll scratch that itch,'

he might have said
before he brought to its knees
a family and an ordinary afternoon.
One shot and another. A calf bawled at a gap.
The birds that scattered from the trees

flew in all directions.

We heard and had to wonder. What was it
came over him? What possessed him
on a given day and not
a million miles from here
to do the like? A whim.

He'd cattle of his own to fodder,
which he did. Then he remembered to give
up himself. 'There's been an accident.
I'll likely need solicitors. You know yourself.
One of those things you have to live

with — if you're let or able.'

Holidays

The night is a sick child.
Fits and starts.
Sheets wringing wet. We eavesdrop
on a troubled dream.
We have come to distant parts

to stay with friends
and wake at last
to the latest news from the North.
A body was found in West Belfast . . . .
The usual backdrop as we break fast.

Far from the land,
we are chewing the cud
of tiredness. He was shot
in the head . . . bound and gagged . . . .
His family objects to the method

of murder. They have lost sight
of the cause.
Down in the harbour
cormorants hang out their wings to dry.
They crashland to their own applause.

Our holiday home's windswept
between a hard rock and a boulder.
We're all at sea. The stars
that should be on Frank's hill
are over my left shoulder.

A Handful of Air

He was ordering drinks across the bar,
a pint and a glass,
his hand held up for the barman
who knew how to decode the signs
of his middle finger and what had to pass

for the one beside it
ever since the morning of the accident.
And later we happened to be drinking
with a friend whose hand was mangled
by the argument

of another machine. And I started to think
about all the dismembered
parts, where they end up — dumped
in a heap, a fire, a furnace, an unmarked
grave. Then something was remembered,

something of the hand found strapped
by a leather belt to the arm
of an armchair in Belfast,
with its handful of air.
Between us and all harm

God help me understand.
Later I learned I'd shaken
hands with a man
who shook hands with an Englishman
whose hand he'd taken

in a letterbomb campaign;
one of the unseen victims,
a name in the papers for a while.
I've had a dream
of a party where the separated limbs

congregate and re-unite — the digits
chiselled at the littlest joint,
the hands hacked off around the wrist . . . .
Something's remembered. Hands hold hands,
fingers are crossed, and the fingers point.

One Day

*There will be milk from the cow
forever; no prices
to pay for a harvest
in every season. No hex. No spell.
There will be no need for sacrifices.*

Now they tell about a well
near here, a hermitage,
where a cripple hauled in on a litter
wandered home on his own steam,
when their whisper broke the pledge

of silence with the story of the woman
with the one and only child.
'Time you were in second gear.'
'Time you went back to the well.'
They didn't know that blood defiled

the prayer of every month. And no,
there wasn't any stir, no touch
that brushed and quickened. They didn't think.
And someone said, 'You mean to say
he hobbled in with a crutch

and sauntered out without . . . . '
I do, and it's true.
'Then what happened to the crutch?'
Someone threw it on the ground.
And one day it grew.

The Wife

She was his wife.
Even he referred
to her as 'my woman'
or 'my other half'.
It never occurred

to some of them that she'd
a name. They knew it all
about her people —
the uncle who got jail,
the cousin who played football

for the county.
She was the one beside
him or stuck at home —
she the shadow, he the sun —
until the day he died.

Then tongues tripped on her christian name.

Omega House

She is glued to her chair
watching another
quiz show on TV
or she's watching a film
she has seen before. Somebody's mother.

She is watching them winning
prize after prize.
She is sick
of the seventeenth 'take'
of their surprise.

Black and white days.
She is driven to tears
by re-runs and re-releases.
Who cares who shot JR?
She is sick — and she has been for years.

She is sick to the teeth
of the compère's smile.
He is driving her slowly
up the wall
she began to defile

with crayons like a child
the day they found
her covered in curtains
she had cut to ribbons
for her hair. The sound

she was making was hardly
her own. Now she promises
to take her pills. She swears.
Pain she knows. It fills
the space of all she misses.

I wish it would be over
soon, she is saying
again. It's so far until evening.
She is looking forward to
the end. She is praying

for that little breeze
that might, just might
nudge her frail craft
a little closer to the harbour
of the long, long night.

Seven Letters Beginning With . . .

'Essence of morphia, compound of cocaine —
If I could only sleep again . . .'
He has drunk himself into the ground
where a want survives, under the weather.
His days on dry land are a hurricane.

Now he's back on an ocean liner
you'd think he might escape —
he has nowhere to go. His library,
his records mean little now.
He has run aground on the cape

of himself.

You might have heard his fortune
on the news at one o'clock — famous
for the first time in his life,
a body out of his brothers' shadow,
broadcast for being anonymous.

In a small hotel in Harcourt Street
with a false name on the register
and travelling light, unsteady feet
on the threadbare pile of the bottom stair,
when the porter greeted, 'Goodnight Mister,'

'It's *Doctor*,' he declared.

'*I* was the physician who couldn't heal
himself.' Oh he'd solve a crossword.
He'd finished *Finnegans Wake*. He'd cure
the captain, crew and passengers. Doctor at sea,
a captain in the army — the fine lines blurred.

'I have no will — I have a wish
my anchor slips
without any pain for anyone and I drift
into a quiet cove where the natives
aren't inquisitive about a ship's

doctor on ship's leave.'

'Season of mists and mellow fruitfulness . . . '
he savours beneath his breath as he stands
at the window in another man's suit
and empties his pockets. Small change.
He must summons himself from the hinterlands

to cover his tracks. No clues.
No traces. The punctilious programme
proceeds — a scalpel excising every tag
and label, a hypodermic needle
unstitching every stitch of a monogram.

He pares away his fingerprints.

Eye to eye with the begetter,
far beyond fear or the thought
of sin, he tightens the tourniquet
and flicks the tip of the syringe.
Essence of morphia . . . Counting to nought

he flexes the muscles of his right thigh.
Compound of cocaine . . . He is humming
the closing bars of a concerto.
He'd be strung on a blackthorn tree
in the *Inferno*. Slowly he's becoming

no one in particular.

D-day. Deadline.
'Oh if only he'd talked
to me, if he hadn't
without as much as a by-your-leave
or a backward look just walked

away, my lost son . . . ' His secret son.
He might never have known the panic
of a man ravenous for a glimmer
of recognition from anyone
whose blind response turned his ways *Titanic*,

his mind *Marie Celeste*.

Easy now. So long waited for,
the desperate remedy
so carefully rehearsed the clock
begins to stop. He's relaxing
like a river eye to eye with the open sea.

Nothing stirs. Wind or wave.
Halcyon days at last, his poise
preserved in the slow wash of the undercurrent
which conducts him to an island
where the trees are fruit and the boys

are friends.

Fast

They missed him in the corner
and, more, his easy money.
For years he'd stared at nothing,
counted cobwebs in the midway air.
Better than being on his own.
And if it cost a packet
for him to lift the latch
what about it? But he'd
not darken their door again.

He saw her pass and left his herd
standing in its stanchions;
she spoke to him, he went weak
in the wits, put his farm in the bank
to buy her what she wanted.
The blind could see that he
was throwing good money after bad.
For she was fast
and friends with many men.

They started soon to say
she'll soon be rambling,
the midnight latch on the door.
They said there'd soon
be separate shopping.
And said they'd soon be living
at both ends of the house.
They said. They said. They said . . .
And they were wrong.

The River

He is whipping the air into shape;
the flies he has tied
drift dry as a bone.
He has taken an element
in his stride.

He is driving them on,
the waterway horses,
flailing the crop of upcountry spawns.
Beneath is the grain. Splashes
are chaff of whitewater courses.

He has stepped into the same stream
often and recently seen it putrefy.
He has loved a place
he'll feel a need to leave.
They had to milk the good cow dry.

He was making light but not little of
the tarnished hallmark
of the bank, the copper line,
dank overgrowth. He was making
light of midsummer dark

when we were fishing and thinking
with a friend. 'There's a lake,'
wrote a man, 'deep
in the mind of everyone,'
and he was making a mistake.

It's a river.

Big

Big as a barndoor. Big
and awkward.
Like a bullock at the bar
at the trough of his own stall,
always and only the bad word

talking to none.
Hard as nails, but soft
in the head. All sulks
and slobbers, and dog rough.
He'd eat hay off a dirty loft.

They were drawing him out,
getting great mileage
out of a row somebody raised
around and about the mess he made
of the second cut of the silage,

the usual boys. And one
was saying, 'You know the way
he'd maybe lend you a hand
at the hay — well he'd charge you
a week and a half for the day'

and that after leaning
since noon on the fork
grumbling for tea and mumbling aloud,
'If I'd left with the others
I'd now be the *Taoiseach* of New York.'

Then he turned on your man
from where he slumped
and grabbed him from behind,
held him in a bear hug,
and humped. Humped.

Silence. Then they started putting chat on him
about all he'd suffered for the Cause,
the blows for Ireland, burning haybarns
and big houses. Wasn't he great?
Oh he was. He was.

He'd count pennies
on the counter of the shop
and peg pounds across the bar,
a small one for himself,
a smoke. He wouldn't stop

to eat except a sister gave him
dinner. You're great, she'd say, just great,
you'd free the nation late at night
but couldn't clear a downpipe in the light
of day. He ate the pattern off her plate.

Winds and Weathers

There are winds and weathers
not noticed
in the daily papers,
forecast or recorded,
the lazy wind that runs
straight through you, or the capers

of a certain blast in County Cavan
not shown on
the television,
on maps or charts,
but earn a mention in the local columns,
a wonder like the risen

Christ. A squall
to skin a goat. Before you'd open
your mouth to speak
it'd lift a haycock
out of the haggard and deposit it
in the middle of next week.

A maverick. A hasky wind.
A hoor. It brings to mind
stories of the snows of '47
when Simons tied his mare to a post
and found it hanging from a steeple
when he came to, a foot from heaven.

Or your father's father's father's tales
of the night of the wind
that raised
the town of Naas — the whole caboosh —
and moved it miles.
Men in the morning gazed

across the Curragh
to find the boots they'd laid
at the bottom of their bed. Local
places learn their local weather.
They've given steady rain on radio,
we've waited for sun or showers. Our focal

point's high over Mullaghmeen.
A major from the Big House
on the battlefields of Burma
planned a countercharge with heed
of his batman from Loughcrew. 'The whites
of their eyes, Sir, wind's from Moylagh!'

Grace

In a matter of months
they will look
straight through you
and be moved — in a matter
of minutes — from hoof to hook.

The waters broke. Some drowned
in air. One of them smothered
under a bale.
One of the mountainy hoggets
mismothered.

Some failed in the fields,
daft lambs, with gid. We've seen
the greycrow beaks
bobbing like the needle
of a *Singer* sewing-machine

leaving empty sockets
like buttonholes
finished in red thread.
They shelter by the ditches
of the dread patrols.

But most of them thrive.
We congregate to eat
at the altar of appetite
and give thanks for our friends,
our children, the good meat.

We know they're each
a lamb and a half, the protegé
of care and mother's milk.
They are taking their ease. Well they might!
They have come a long way.

A Way of the World

A lost light shines
in the haggard
of years. So much begins,
like a pearl, upon a blemish.
Some take life hard,

some take the same life
easy. I'd sooner sing
heartbreak nor cry it.
But a baby's born, the baby
dies. Who knows anything?

The World of Women

She whispers 'Stay'.
You lie by her side.
You touch the silk
bandages.
          Resist the will
to caress her breast.
It will fill
into a fortune of milk
for the baby who died
on Saturday.

A Part of Ourselves

Forewarned but not forearmed —
no, not for this.
A word first whispered months ago
and longed for longer tripped on the tongue,
a stammer, now a broken promise.

Averted eyes. Uncertain talk
of a certain strange condition.
The scanned screen slips out of focus,
a lunar scene, granite shapes, shifting.
We bent beneath the weight of attrition

knowing it might have been worse.

We were visited.
Now the minutes are grief
or grief postponed — not to remember
seems to betray; laughter would be sacrilege.
We will find a way to mind him as a leaf

who fell already from the family tree,
crushed. He hadn't a chance.
We pray at best for the open wound
to grow a scar.
We welcome him his deliverance.

There are things worse than death.

Imagine a man not wanting to live
who could. Now he lies in an oxygen tent
in the whispered kindness of nurses.
Night and day are one to him,
his without hunger, just bewilderment

and quiet uncomplaining. Brightly lit.
He seems to breathe another air.
There's a photograph in *The Best of* LIFE:
A summary execution, Budapest, October 1956.
He flinched that way from the snapshot glare

of the world laid out for him.

So they gave her sedatives.
I sought and found the comfort of a friend.
She tendered brave communion
in the early hours
as I waited, waited, for the given end.

There are more hurts than cures.
Already we'd begun talking
the hushed courtesies of loss.
Then, at dawn, the telephone.
It seems I've been sleepwalking

since.

We broached the sorrow hoard
of women, tales unmentioned in their marriages,
unsaid to friends, to families.
Fellow feeling loosed their tongues
about unwanted pregnancies, abortions, miscarriages,

as his remains, a fingerful of hair,
a photograph, his cold kiss called, 'Remember me,'
and I stood with them at the lip
of graves. She cried from miles away,
'I miss my baby,' as an amputee

laments a phantom limb.

Time and again, for years on years,
I've thought about a corner of Loughcrew,
a three-foot plot for 'Henry Timson,
born and died September 2nd, 1899',
sheltered under ivy-overgrown yew,

and wondered how you'd walk away from burying
a child. Little I knew. Now the sound
of a cousin's prayers and Pa Grimes' spade
wheels me round and her sudden, 'We are leaving
a part of ourselves in that ground.'

The innocent part.

He'll die again at Christmas every year.
We felt the need grow all night
to give him a name, to assert him
as a member of our care, to say he was
alive. Oh, he lived all right,

he lived a lifetime. Now certain sounds,
sights and smells are the shibboleth
of a season. In a hospital corridor
I held him in my arms. I held him tight.
His mother and I, we held our breath —

and he held his.

Acknowledgements

Jarlath Hayes's cover illustration is based on a photograph, 'Loughcrew, formal garden: view through arch to temple, c. 1860'. Acknowledgements are due to The Irish Architectural Archive.

I acknowledge gratefully the welcome accorded to some of these poems by the editors of Book Arts (U. of Alabama, Tuscaloosa), *The Cavan Leader*, *Éire-Ireland*, *Erect Me a Monument of Broken Wings*, *The Irish Times*, *North Dakota Quarterly*, The Pinchpenny Press, *Poetry Canada Review*, *The Simon Anthology of Poetry* and *Quarry* (Canada).

Some of them were completed at the Tyrone Guthrie Centre, Annaghmakerrig. Several were included in *The Poet's Voice* (RTE). 'Windfalls' appeared first in *Hill Field*, a Festschrift for John Montague. 'The River' is dedicated to Barrie Cooke, and to Jean Valentine, for Barrie's 60th birthday. *Remembering*, a novel by Wendell Berry, was at the back of my mind as I was writing 'A Handful of Air'. Wendell's supreme example remains a guiding light.